DURGA – THE SLAYER OF MAHISHA

THE ASURA, MAHISHA, ONCE PERFORMED SEVERE PENANCES TO PROPITIATE BRAHMA. PLEASED WITH HIS AUSTERITIES, BRAHMA APPEARED BEFORE HIM.

LORD, MAKE ME IMMORTAL.

ALL WHO ARE BORN MUST DIE. YOU CANNOT ESCAPE DEATH.

MAHISHA BECAME THOUGHTFUL.

WHAT SHALL I DO? HAVE I PERFORMED ALL THOSE PENANCES FOR NOTHING? AH! I HAVE IT!

1

2

A LITTLE LATER, INDRA RUSHED OUT OF AMARAVATI, HIS CAPITAL.

YOU CAN'T GO ANY FARTHER, O MAHISHA. TURN BACK. YOU'VE TRIED TIME AND AGAIN TO TAKE AMARAVATI AND HAVE FAILED. WHY DO YOU PERSIST?

INDRA, I'VE COME TO FIGHT, NOT TO TALK. USE YOUR WEAPONS INSTEAD OF YOUR TONGUE!

STUNG BY MAHISHA'S WORDS, INDRA DARTED FORWARD BRANDISHING HIS WEAPON — THE THUNDERBOLT.

ATTACK, O DEVAS. LET NO ASURA ESCAPE.

THEN ENSUED A FIERCE BATTLE BETWEEN THE DEVAS AND THE ASURAS.

SEVERELY BEATEN, THE DEVAS HAD TO RUN FOR THEIR LIVES.

AFTER DRIVING THE DEVAS OUT OF AMARAVATI, MAHISHA ASCENDED INDRA'S THRONE.

I AM THE LORD OF LORDS. HENCEFORTH I ALONE SHALL BE WORSHIPPED. THE WORSHIP OF BRAHMA, VISHNU AND SHIVA SHOULD BE STOPPED FORTHWITH.

MAHISHA'S MEN BEGAN TO HARASS THOSE PIOUS MEN WHO CONTINUED TO WORSHIP VISHNU OR SHIVA.

WORSHIP MAHISHA OR DIE!

REPLACE THAT SHIVA-LINGA* WITH AN IDOL OF MAHISHA! OR ELSE...

O GOD OF GODS! WHEN WILL YOU SAVE US FROM THIS PLIGHT?

* A FORM IN WHICH SHIVA IS WORSHIPPED

MEANWHILE, UNKNOWN TO THEM, THE DEVAS HAD ALREADY ASSEMBLED AT KAILAS, THE ABODE OF LORD SHIVA.

WE ARE HELPLESS AGAINST MAHISHA. WILL EVIL TRIUMPH OVER RIGHT-EOUSNESS?

EVEN AS THE DEVAS SPOKE, AN INTENSE LIGHT ISSUED FORTH FROM THE ENRAGED FACES OF SHIVA, VISHNU AND BRAHMA.

IT WAS JOINED BY SIMILAR RAYS OF LIGHT FROM INDRA AND OTHER DEVAS. AND LO! THE NEXT MOMENT, OUT OF THAT LIGHT A FEMALE FORM WITH A THOUSAND ARMS CAME INTO BEING! IT WAS DEVI DURGA.

ARMED WITH THE CELESTIAL WEAPONS AND MOUNTED ON A LION, DURGA EMITTED A BLOOD-CURDLING ROAR.

I'LL SEEK OUT AND DESTROY THE EVIL MAHISHA.

THE SEAS TREMBLED...

...THE EARTH SHOOK AND THE MOUNTAINS ROCKED.

MAHISHA'S HEART MISSED A BEAT.

WHAT'S THAT?

HE RUSHED OUT OF HIS PALACE TO FIND OUT.

HO! A MERE FEMALE!

NO! I AM NO MERE FEMALE! I HAVE COME TO FULFIL BRAHMA'S BOON. YOU WANTED TO DIE AT THE HANDS OF A WOMAN, DIDN'T YOU?

MAHISHA HASTILY STEPPED BACK AND CALLED TO HIS MEN.

GET HER! KILL HER!

AS THE ASURAS HURLED VARIOUS WEAPONS AT HER, DURGA BREATHED HARD.

AS SHE BREATHED, THOUSANDS OF SOLDIERS CAME INTO BEING AND FOUGHT AT HER SIDE.

HER MOUNT STRODE THROUGH MAHISHA'S ARMY, DESTROYING THOUSANDS OF ASURAS.

MAHISHA SEETHED WITH FURY.

I'LL ANNIHILATE THIS MONSTER AND HER HORDES.

ASSUMING THE FORM OF A BUFFALO, MAHISHA CHARGED FORTH SNORTING AND BELLOWING.

HE TRAMPLED UPON DURGA'S MEN . . .

. . . AND LASHED AT THEM WITH HIS TAIL .

ENRAGED, DURGA FLUNG A NOOSE AT HIM.

MAHISHA SHOOK HIMSELF WITH ALL HIS MIGHT . . .

. . . TRANSFORMED HIMSELF INTO A LION AND POUNCED UPON DURGA.

AS DURGA CHOPPED OFF THE HEAD OF THE LION . . .

. . . MAHISHA ROSE IN HIS OWN FORM AND CHARGED.

LATER HE ASSUMED THE FORM OF AN ELEPHANT AND TUGGED AT DURGA'S MOUNT WITH HIS TRUNK.

DURGA LOPPED OFF THE TRUNK WITH HER SWORD.

MAHISHA AGAIN ASSUMED THE FORM OF A BUFFALO AND SNORTED WITH RAGE.

DURGA LOOKED AT HIM WITH CONTEMPT.

SNORT, O FOOL! IN A MOMENT, THE DEVAS WILL ROAR IN TRIUMPH AT THIS VERY PLACE, WHEN YOU ARE SLAIN!

ENRAGED, MAHISHA RUSHED AT HER.

BUT DURGA LEAPT UPON HIM AND PINNED HIM DOWN.

MAHISHA STRUGGLED TO FREE HIMSELF. AS HALF OF HIM EMERGED FROM THE MOUTH OF THE BUFFALO, DURGA RAISED HER SWORD.

THE NEXT MOMENT, MAHISHA FELL DEAD, AT THE FOOT OF DURGA. THE DEVAS WERE OVERJOYED.

O DURGA, UPHOLDER OF VIRTUE, DESTROYER OF EVIL, WE HUMBLY SALUTE YOU! O DEVI, CONTINUE TO PROTECT US!

CHAMUNDI

ON ANOTHER OCCASION, THE DEVAS WERE DRIVEN OUT OF HEAVEN BY SHUMBHA, THE LORD OF THE ASURAS.

CHANDA AND MUNDA, SHUMBHA'S COMMANDERS, FOLLOWED THE DEVAS.

LET'S FIND OUT WHERE THEY GO AND WHY.

THE DEVAS WENT TO MOUNT HIMAVAT AND PRAYED TO DURGA.

O DURGA, PROTECTOR OF THE VIRTUOUS, DESTROY THE EVIL SHUMBHA AND RESTORE RIGHTEOUSNESS.

JUST THEN PARVATI, SHIVA'S CONSORT, WHO WAS ON HER WAY TO THE RIVER, HAPPENED TO PASS BY.

AND LO! THE NEXT MOMENT, GODDESS AMBIKA* SPRANG FORTH FROM THE BODY OF PARVATI.

WHAT A BREATH-TAKING BEAUTY! WE SHOULD INFORM SHUMBHA.

LET'S RUN TO OUR MASTER.

WHEN CHANDA AND MUNDA RUSH-ED TO THE PALACE OF SHUMBHA AND DESCRIBED AMBIKA TO HIM.

THAT BEAUTIFUL ONE SHALL BE MINE! BRING HER TO ME!

* AN INCARNATION OF DURGA

CHANDA AND MUNDA RUSHED BACK TO MOUNT HIMAVAT.

O BEAUTIFUL ONE, SHUMBHA THE LORD OF THE THREE WORLDS WHO POSSESSES UNEQUALLED WEALTH WANTS TO MARRY YOU.

I'VE TAKEN A VOW THAT I'LL MARRY ONLY HIM WHO CAN CONQUER ME IN BATTLE AND HUMBLE MY PRIDE.

DO YOU SEEK TO BATTLE WITH THE GREAT ASURA WHO HAS VANQUISHED EVEN THE DEVAS? BE WISE AND SUBMIT GRACEFULLY TO OUR MASTER.

I KNOW I AM FOOLISH BUT I AM BOUND BY THE ILL-CONSIDERED VOW TAKEN LONG AGO.

WE'LL INFORM OUR MASTER.

WHEN CHANDA AND MUNDA CONVEYED AMBIKA'S MESSAGE TO SHUMBHA —

IF IT'S BATTLE SHE WANTS, SHE SHALL HAVE IT.

THEN HE TURNED TO ANOTHER OF HIS COMMANDERS, DHUMRALOCHANA.

GO, AND BRING HER TO ME.

DHUMRALOCHANA TOOK AN ARMY TO MOUNT HIMAVAT AND CONFRONTED AMBIKA.

IF YOU DON'T GO TO MY LORD, OF YOUR OWN FREE WILL, I'LL HAVE TO TAKE YOU TO HIM BY FORCE.

AMBIKA PRETENDED TO BE AFRAID.

ALAS! SPARE ME. I AM A HELPLESS WOMAN.

THEN MARRY OUR LORD!

MY VOW DOES NOT PERMIT ME TO MARRY HIM WITHOUT FIGHTING HIM.

WITHOUT WASTING ANOTHER WORD, DHUMRALOCHANA RUSHED TOWARDS HER.

WITH UTTER CONTEMPT FOR THE ASURA, AMBIKA UTTERED A SINGLE SYLLABLE.

HUM!

THE NEXT MOMENT, A HANDFUL OF ASHES SMOULDERED WHERE THE MIGHTY ASURA ONCE STOOD.

FLEE!

FLEE!

BUT CHANDA AND MUNDA STOPPED THE RETREATING ASURAS.

OUR LORD HAS ORDERED US TO CAPTURE THIS VILLAINOUS WOMAN. SHE IS ONE, WE ARE MANY. DO NOT GIVE UP. WE'LL SURROUND HER AND SEIZE HER.

WHEN THE ASURAS CLOSED IN ON AMBIKA, WHO WAS NOW SEATED ON A LION...

...SHE FROWNED.

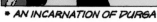

* AN INCARNATION OF DURGA

OUT CAME KALI* FROM HER FOREHEAD...

...AND CHARGED AT THE ASURAS.

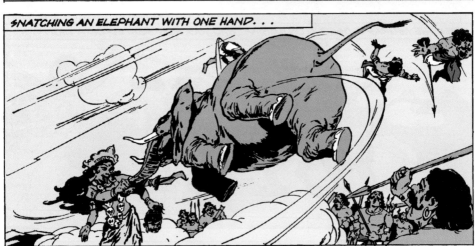

SNATCHING AN ELEPHANT WITH ONE HAND...

...SHE HURLED IT AT THE ASURAS AND CRUSHED THEM TO DEATH.

CHANDA RUSHED AT KALI.

I WILL KILL YOU AND PROVIDE A FEAST FOR THE VULTURES!

KALI SEIZED HIM BY THE HAIR...

...AND BEHEADED HIM.

BLIND WITH FURY, MUNDA RUSHED FORTH.

...ONLY TO MEET WITH THE SAME FATE!

AMBIKA SMILED AT KALI.

YOU HAVE KILLED CHANDA AND MUNDA. HENCEFORTH YOU SHALL ALSO BE KNOWN AS CHAMUNDI.

HOW DURGA SLEW SHUMBHA

WHEN SHUMBHA LEARNED THAT CHANDA AND MUNDA HAD BEEN KILLED, HE CAME IN PERSON TO DEAL WITH AMBIKA. HIS HUGE ARMY SURROUNDED AMBIKA AND KALI.

THEN THE SHAKTIS — THE INNER FORCE OF VARIOUS GODS — ISSUED FORTH ASSUMING FEMALE FORMS: OUT OF BRAHMA EMERGED BRAHMANI...

* EACH OF THESE FORMS IS CONSIDERED TO BE AN INCARNATION OF DURGA.

...OUT OF VISHNU, VAISHNAVI...

...AND OUT OF MAHESHWARA, MAHESHWARI.

FINALLY OUT OF AMBIKA EMERGED CHANDIKA. SOON THE SKY WAS FILLED WITH HUNDREDS OF SHAKTIS.*

IN THE GREAT BATTLE THAT FOLLOWED, BRAHMANI SPRINKLED WATER FROM HER KAMANDALU ON THE ENEMIES, MAKING THEM WEAK AND INERT.

* SHAKTI = ENERGY

VAISHNAVI FOUGHT WITH THE DISCUS , MAHESHWARI WITH THE TRIDENT, AND VARIOUS OTHER SHAKTIS WITH THEIR RESPECTIVE WEAPONS. UNABLE TO FACE THIS ONSLAUGHT, THE ASURAS BEGAN TO FLEE.

FLEEING FROM WOMEN ! SHAME ON YOU ! TURN ROUND AND FIGHT.

IT WAS THE TERRIBLE ASURA, RAKTABEEJA.

AS RAKTABEEJA RUSHED FORTH, INDRA'S SHAKTI STRUCK HIM WITH HER THUNDERBOLT.

AS EACH DROP OF THE BLOOD FLOWING FROM HIS WOUND TOUCHED THE GROUND . . .

...THERE ROSE A MIGHTY ASURA, HIS EXACT REPLICA...

...TO FIGHT THE SHAKTIS.

AS THE SHAKTIS WOUNDED EACH OF THE ASURAS THUS BORN, OUT OF HIS BLOOD ROSE MANY MORE ASURAS...

...AND SOON THE BATTLE SCENE WAS FILLED WITH THOUSANDS OF RAKTA-BEEJAS, WHO FOUGHT THE SHAKTIS.

CHANDIKA TURNED TO KALI.

O CHAMUNDI, THESE RAKTA-BEEJAS CAN BE ANNIHILATED ONLY IF WE PREVENT THEIR BLOOD FROM FALLING TO THE GROUND.

LEAVE IT TO ME. NOT A DROP OF THEIR BLOOD SHALL STAIN THE EARTH AGAIN.

AS CHANDIKA AND THE OTHER SHAKTIS ATTACKED THE RAKTABEEJAS...

...KALI PREVENTED THE BIRTH OF ANY MORE ASURAS.

SOON THE HUNDREDS AND THOUSANDS OF RAKTABEEJAS THAT HAD ARISEN WERE WIPED OUT. RAKTABEEJA WAS FURIOUS.

I MUST KILL HER BEFORE SHE STRIKES THE FATAL BLOW.

AND RAKTABEEJA RUSHED TOWARDS CHANDIKA.

AS CHANDIKA STRUCK HIM . . .

. . . KALI PREVENTED HIS BLOOD FROM TOUCHING THE EARTH . . .

. . . AND RAKTABEEJA FELL DEAD, TO THE JOY OF THE DEVAS.

VICTORY TO CHANDIKA !

SHUMBHA AND HIS BROTHER NISHUMBHA WERE STUNNED WHEN THEY HEARD THE NEWS.

NISHUMBHA, YOU ALONE ARE CAPABLE OF KILLING HER.

I'LL TAKE HER ON, BROTHER.

BUT THE MOST POWERFUL ASURA, NISHUMBHA, WAS NO MATCH FOR CHANDIKA.

ALAS! MY BROTHER IS DEAD!

O DURGA, THERE IS NO GLORY IN YOUR VICTORY. HELPED BY OTHERS, YOU'VE DESTROYED MY MEN.

I AM ALONE. THE GODDESSES YOU SEE ARE BUT DIFFERENT FORMS OF MYSELF.

THEN TO THE AMAZEMENT OF SHUMBHA, THE VARIOUS SHAKTIS MERGED INTO DURGA.

SEIZING DURGA, SHUMBHA ROSE INTO THE SKY.

AFTER A FIERCE BATTLE IN MID-AIR, DURGA FLUNG THE ASURA DOWN . . .

. . . AND SLEW HIM WITH HER SPEAR. REJOICING, THE DEVAS HEADED BY INDRA APPEARED ON THE SCENE.

WE SALUTE YOU, O MOTHER DURGA, DESTROYER OF EVIL.

CELEBRATING

50

AMAR
CHITRA
KATHA

YEARS

It was in 1967 that the first Amar Chitra Katha comic rolled off the presses, changing story-telling for children across India forever.

Five decades and more than 400 books later, we are still sharing stories from India's rich heritage, primarily because of the love and support shown by readers like yourself.

SO, FROM US TO YOU, HERE'S A BIG
THANK YOU!

SATI AND SHIVA

The route to your roots

SATI AND SHIVA

Only Sati could fulfill Shiva's exacting demands. As his companion she could match his ascetic ways as well as be a loving wife. Unfortunately, her happiness was overshadowed by an arrogant father. Sati countered Daksha's insensitivity with an immense, horrific sacrifice, which threw the universe into chaos and turmoil. As the heroine of this primeval romantic story she embodies the essence of a perfect spouse.

Script
Kamala Chandrakant

Illustrations
P.B.Kavadi

Editor
Anant Pai

Cover illustration by: Dayal Patkar

SATI AND SHIVA

BRAHMA WANTED THE ASCETIC SHIVA TO GET MARRIED. VISHNU ADVISED HIM TO SERVE THE GODDESS UMA, BEG HER TO TAKE BIRTH ON EARTH, AND BECOME SHIVA'S CONSORT.

BRAHMA DID AS HE WAS ADVISED AND UMA WAS BORN TO HIS SON—THE CHIEF PRAJAPATI, DAKSHA.

SHE SHALL BE CALLED SATI.

EVEN AS A YOUNG GIRL, SATI WAS A STAUNCH DEVOTEE OF SHIVA.

WHERE IS SATI?

THERE. BUSY AS USUAL SINGING SONGS IN PRAISE OF LORD SHIVA.

SATI SOON GREW UP.

HOW BEAUTIFUL OUR DAUGHTER IS. SHE SHOULD BE GIVEN IN MARRIAGE TO ONE WHO IS HER EQUAL.

ONLY THE WORTHIEST ONE IN ALL THE THREE WORLDS SHALL BECOME HER HUSBAND.

A FEW DAYS LATER, BRAHMA AND THE SAGE NARADA CAME TO VISIT DAKSHA.

MY CHILD, PAY OBEISANCE TO THE REVERED ONES.

2

MAY THE MIGHTY SHIVA, WHOM YOU ADORE, BE YOUR LORD. HE HAS NOT TAKEN AND WILL NEVER TAKE ANOTHER CONSORT.

I SHALL PERFORM SEVERE PENANCES AND WIN MY LORD.

SHE BEGAN BY FASTING AND CHANTING SACRED MANTRAS.

THEN, IN DRIPPING WET CLOTHES, SHE WORSHIPPED HIM ON THE BANK OF A RIVER.

MY LORD, COME TO ME AND FULFIL MY DESTINY.

HER WHOLE BEING WAS CONCENTRATED ON SHIVA. SHE KNEW NOTHING ELSE.

3

MEANWHILE IN HEAVEN— SATI HAS BEGUN HER PENANCES TO WIN SHIVA.

LET US GO AND BLESS HER.

SO BRAHMA AND HIS CONSORT SARASWATI, VISHNU AND HIS CONSORT LAKSHMI, AND THE CELESTIAL SAGES CAME TO SATI. BUT—

SHE IS OBLIVIOUS TO US. SO DEEP IS HER CONCENTRATION. IT IS DIVINE.

THEY WHO HAD COME TO BLESS HER SOUGHT HER BLESSINGS, INSTEAD.

THEN THEY WENT TO SHIVA.

O SHIVA, YOU TOO ACCEPT A LOVING WOMAN FOR AN ETERNAL COMPANION AS VISHNU HAS TAKEN LAKSHMI, AND I, SARASWATI.

SHIVA SMILED AND WAS QUIET FOR SOME TIME. THEN—

I AM WILLING TO MARRY. BUT I AM AN ASCETIC.

IS THERE A WOMAN WHO WILL BE A YOGINI WHEN I PRACTISE YOGA AND A LOVING HOUSE-WIFE WHEN I AM A HOUSEHOLDER?

5

BRAHMA WAS DELIGHTED.

O SHIVA, SATI, MY GRAND-DAUGHTER IS ONE SUCH.

YES SHIVA, SHE IS!

WHERE IS SHE?

AT THIS MOMENT SHE IS ENGAGED IN SEVERE PENANCES TO WIN YOU. HER CONCENTRATION IS UNSWERVING.

THEN VISHNU PLEADED.

O SHIVA, GRANT HER THE BOON SHE SEEKS AND MARRY HER.

SO BE IT!

THEIR MISSION ACCOMPLISHED, BRAHMA, VISHNU AND THE REST DEPARTED.

I SHALL GO TO SATI.

THOUGH SHIVA KNEW WHAT THE BOON WOULD BE, HE WANTED TO HEAR HER SPEAK.

HOW CAN I TELL HIM THAT HE IS THE BOON I SEEK?

SATI HESITATED BUT FOR A SECOND. THEN—

LORD, WILL YOU...

BUT SHIVA DID NOT LET HER COMPLETE HER QUESTION.

BE MY CONSORT, SATI.

FOR A WHILE SATI STOOD SMILING SWEETLY AT HIM. THEN—

LORD, PLEASE TAKE ME WITH THE CONSENT AND THE BLESSINGS OF MY FATHER.

SO BE IT!

WHEN SHIVA REACHED KAILAS, HE SENT FOR BRAHMA.

I HAVE GRANTED SATI THE BOON SHE SOUGHT. NOW YOU GO AND SPEAK TO DAKSHA.

BRAHMA SUCCEEDED IN PERSUADING DAKSHA.

LET HIM COME TO ME ON AN AUSPICIOUS DAY AND I SHALL OFFER HIM MY DAUGHTER.

AND SATI WAS MARRIED TO SHIVA.

AFTER THE WEDDING, SHIVA TOOK SATI TO KAILAS WHERE THEY SPENT MANY A HAPPY DAY.

THEN ONE DAY—

THE SAGES AT PRAYAG ARE PERFORMING A GRAND YAGNA. ALL THE CELESTIAL BEINGS HAVE BEEN INVITED. WOULD YOU LIKE TO GO?

I WOULD, MY LORD!

SO SHIVA AND SATI WENT.

9

WHEN THEY ENTERED THE GROUNDS, THE DEVAS AND SAGES BOWED TO THEM.

COME, SATI. LET US SIT AT THE PLACE ASSIGNED TO US.

AS SOON AS THEY WERE SEATED, DAKSHA ENTERED.

HA! THEY RECOGNISE ME AS THE CHIEF PRAJAPATI.

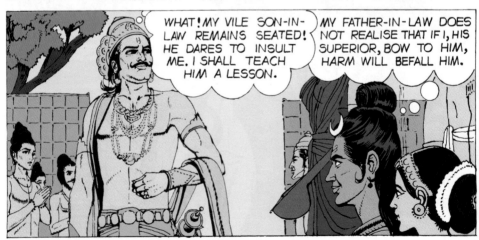

WHAT! MY VILE SON-IN-LAW REMAINS SEATED! HE DARES TO INSULT ME. I SHALL TEACH HIM A LESSON.

MY FATHER-IN-LAW DOES NOT REALISE THAT IF I, HIS SUPERIOR, BOW TO HIM, HARM WILL BEFALL HIM.

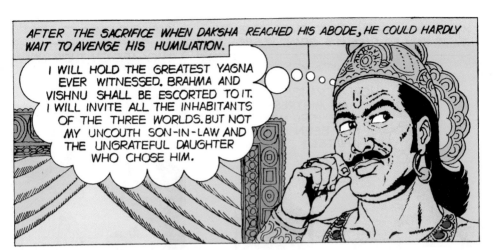

11

WHEN SHE LEARNT THAT THEY WERE ON THEIR WAY TO DAKSHA'S GRAND YAGNA—

HOW STRANGE THAT MY MISTRESS AND THE LORD HAVE NOT BEEN INVITED!

SHE RETURNED TO SATI.

THEY ARE ON THEIR WAY TO A GRAND YAGNA, YOUR FATHER IS PERFORMING.

MY FATHER?

SATI WAS SURPRISED.

HOW COULD FATHER FORGET TO INVITE US?

SHE WENT TO SHIVA AND TOLD HIM ABOUT THE SACRIFICE.

LET US GO TO MY FATHER'S SACRIFICIAL HALL.

SO SATI SET OUT ON NANDI, SHIVA'S FAVOURITE ATTENDANT.

AT THE GATES OF DAKSHA'S ABODE, SATI DISMOUNTED AND WALKED UP TO HER FATHER. BUT HE IGNORED HER PRESENCE.

YET SATI, EVER DUTIFUL, BOWED TO HER PARENTS.

THEN —

WHY WERE MY LORD AND I NOT INVITED?

WHEN DAKSHA DID NOT REPLY, SHE TURNED UPON VISHNU AND BRAHMA.

HOW COULD YOU TOLERATE THIS INSULT TO MY LORD? YOU WHO···

BUT DAKSHA CRUELLY CUT HER SHORT.

SATI! I'VE HAD ENOUGH OF YOUR IMPUDENCE. YOU MAY GO OR STAY. WHY DID YOU COME AT ALL?

HIS ANGER MOUNTED AS HE SPOKE OF SHIVA.

YOUR HUSBAND IS UNCOUTH. HE IS NOT FIT TO BE PRESENT ON SUCH AN AUSPICIOUS OCCASION. I GAVE YOU TO HIM ONLY BECAUSE MY FATHER PERSUADED ME TO.

THEN HE BECAME CALMER.

ANYWAY, NOW THAT YOU HAVE COME, FORGET HIM. SIT DOWN AND ACCEPT A SHARE OF THE SACRIFICIAL OFFERINGS.

SATI, FOR A MOMENT, STOOD SPEECHLESS WITH SHAME AND ANGER.

WHY? OH WHY DID I INSIST ON COMING?

THEN SHE TURNED UPON HER FATHER.

YOU ARE VAIN AND WICKED. I AM ASHAMED TO CALL MYSELF YOUR DAUGHTER.

I WILL CAST OFF THIS BODY OF MINE AS A WORTHLESS CORPSE.

THEN, BECOMING CALMER, SHE FIXED HER MIND ON HER LORD.

MY LORD, I SHALL COME BACK TO YOU WHEN I AM RE-BORN OF A FATHER I CAN RESPECT.

AND INVOKING YOGIC FLAMES, SATI IMMOLATED HER BODY IN THEM.

ALAS! SHIVA'S BELOVED HAS GIVEN UP HER BODY.

ALAS!

ALAS!

CRUEL DAKSHA WILL HAVE TO PAY FOR THIS.

HER ATTENDANTS, WHO WERE WAITING OUTSIDE, HEARD THESE CRIES AND CHARGED IN.

FIE ON THE EVIL PRAJAPATI!

WHERE IS HE?

A TERRIBLE FIGHT ENSUED.

SHIVA'S ATTENDANTS WERE DEFEATED...

...AND HAD TO RETREAT.

...DASHED IT TO THE GROUND.

BOOM

THE CLUSTER SPLIT IN TWO.

FROM ONE HALF AROSE THE POWERFUL VIRABHADRA AND...

...FROM THE OTHER THE TERRIBLE MAHAKALI.

LORD, COMMAND ME QUICKLY! WHAT AM I TO DO?

MAY VICTORY BE YOURS.

DESTROY THE SACRIFICE OF THE CONCEITED DAKSHA. KILL HIM AND RETURN. TAKE AS MANY OF MY ATTENDANTS AS YOU NEED.

EAGER TO CARRY OUT THE COMMAND, VIRABHADRA SET OFF AT ONCE FOR DAKSHA'S ABODE WITH MAHAKALI LEADING THE HORDES.

DAKSHA APPEALED TO INDRA, KING OF THE DEVAS.

I NOW DEPEND ON YOUR STRENGTH AND SUPPORT ALONE. SAVE MY SACRIFICE AND MY LIFE.

INDRA IMMEDIATELY MOUNTED HIS ELEPHANT AND LED THE DEVAS.

MANY OF THE DEVAS AND CELESTIAL SAGES DESERTED AND FLED TO HEAVEN.

OUR RACE WILL BE WIPED OUT. LET US FLEE.

BUT INDRA DID NOT GIVE UP. HE ATTACKED NANDI.

NANDI PIERCED HIM WITH HIS TRIDENT.

INDRA RETALIATED WITH HIS THUNDERBOLT, AND NANDI FELL.

VIRABHADRA WAS FURIOUS TO SEE SHIVA'S FAVOURITE LYING UNCONSCIOUS.

HE DREW HIS BOW AND LET FLY HIS DEADLY ARROWS.

SEVERELY WOUNDED, EVEN INDRA HAD TO FLEE.

LOOK! OUR LEADER IS RETREATING. WE ARE LOST.

THEN VISHNU CAME FORWARD, TOOK INDRA'S POSITION AND FACED VIRABHADRA.

BUT VIRABHADRA CHARGED WITH HIS TRIDENT AND VISHNU FELL UNCONSCIOUS.

LEAVING HIM THERE, VIRABHADRA WENT IN SEARCH OF DAKSHA.

HA! THERE YOU ARE, EVIL ONE!

HE TORE OFF DAKSHA'S HEAD AND...

...THREW IT INTO THE SACRIFICIAL FIRE.

HIS TASK ACCOMPLISHED, HE RETURNED TO KAILAS.

AS VIRABHADRA LEFT, COOL FRAGRANT BREEZES BLEW, REVIVING ALL THOSE WHO HAD FALLEN.

BRAHMA CAME UP TO VISHNU.

MY SON MUST BE BROUGHT TO LIFE AND THE YAGNA COMPLETED. WHAT SHOULD WE DO?

LET'S GO TO SHIVA'S ABODE AND PROPITIATE HIM.

WHEN THEY REACHED SHIVA'S ABODE ON MOUNT KAILAS —

GREAT ONE! YOU ARE MERCIFUL. LET THE INCOMPLETE YAGNA OF DAKSHA BE COMPLETED. LET HIM BE RESTORED TO LIFE.

DAKSHA ALLOWED HATE TO BECOME HIS MASTER. IF ONE HATES ANOTHER IT WILL RECOIL ON ONESELF. DAKSHA SHALL BE REVIVED, BUT WITH THE HEAD OF A GOAT.

THEN COME TO THE SACRIFICIAL ALTAR WITH US, O LORD.

I SHALL.

30

WHEN THEY REACHED THE VENUE OF THE SACRIFICE—

BRING ME THE HEAD OF THE SACRIFICIAL GOAT.

THE HEAD WAS BROUGHT. SHIVA JOINED IT TO DAKSHA'S NECK

DAKSHA SLOWLY AROSE AS IF FROM A DEEP SLEEP.

WHEN HE SAW SHIVA, HE BOWED BEFORE HIM.

I HAVE BEEN WICKED AND FOOLISH. YOU HAVE PUNISHED ME. I PRAY NOW THAT I BE PERMITTED TO COMPLETE MY YAGNA.

WITH SHIVA'S PERMISSION AND GRACIOUS BLESSINGS, DAKSHA COMPLETED THE YAGNA.

AT KAILAS, SHIVA WENT INTO MEDIATATION TILL···

···SATI, TRUE TO HER WORD, WAS REBORN AS PARVATI TO HIMAVAN, A FATHER SHE COULD LOVE AND RESPECT AND WHO LOVED AND RESPECTED HER. AND AS PARVATI SHE WOOED AND WON SHIVA, NEVER TO BE SEPARATED FROM HIM AGAIN.

SHIVA PARVATI

The route to your roots

SHIVA PARVATI

A powerful demon threatens the gods in their heaven. They need a saviour, who, Lord Brahma decrees, will be the son born to Shiva and Parvati. But Shiva – a badly-dressed, untidy, solitary ascetic – seems to enjoy bachelorhood. Even Parvati's unmatched beauty aided by Kama, the god of love, seems unequal to the task of enchanting the stern lord.

This illustrated classic is based on Kumara Sambhava of Kalidasa.

Script	Illustrations	Editor
Kamala Chandrakant	Ram Waeerkar	Anant Pai

SHIVA PARVATI

SHIVA'S FATHER-IN-LAW, DAKSHA, FOR SOME REASON DISLIKED HIM AND NEVER LOST AN OPPORTUNITY TO INSULT HIM. SATI, SHIVA'S WIFE, ASHAMED OF BEING THE DAUGHTER OF SUCH A FATHER, GAVE UP HER BODY. AFTER SATI'S DEATH, SHIVA WENT BACK TO HIS MEDITATION ON THE HIMALAYAS.

VERY NEAR THE GROVE WHERE SHIVA MEDITATED, LIVED THE GREAT MOUNTAIN KING, HIMAVAT.

HE HAD MARRIED THE HEAVENLY NYMPH MENAKA.

THEY WERE LOVED DEARLY BY ALL.

ONE DAY —

MENAKA HAS HAD A BABY GIRL! A LOVELY CHILD!

LET US CALL HER PARVATI.

NATURE TOO REJOICED AT PARVATI'S BIRTH.

WHAT A BEAUTIFUL CHILD SHE IS!

HUSH! DO NOT PROVOKE THE EVIL SPIRITS.

PARVATI WAS REALLY SATI WHO HAD BEEN REBORN, BUT THIS TIME TO A FATHER SHE COULD BE PROUD OF AND WHO WAS PROUD OF HER.

SHE WAS AS LIVELY AS SHE WAS LOVELY AND HAD MANY FRIENDS.

PARVATI! CATCH HA! HA! YOU MISSED AGAIN.

I HAVE HAD ENOUGH OF THIS GAME. COME LET US GO HOME AND PLAY WITH OUR DOLLS.

THE YEARS FLEW BY AND PARVATI GREW UP TO BE A BEAUTIFUL MAIDEN.

PARVATI, MY CHILD, IT IS TIME YOU WERE MARRIED!

MOTHER!

THAT NIGHT—

IT IS HIGH TIME WE FOUND A HUSBAND FOR PARVATI.

I KNOW. BUT I CANNOT THINK OF ANY ONE WORTHY ENOUGH.

HIMAVAT DOTED ON HIS DAUGHTER. ONLY THE BEST WAS GOOD ENOUGH FOR HER.

I WILL GIVE MY PEERLESS CHILD TO ONE WORTHY OF HER IN EVERY RESPECT.

ONE DAY THE SAGE NARADA VISITED HIMAVAT.

NARAYANA! NARAYANA!

PARVATI! COME HERE.

COMING, FATHER.

WHEN PARVATI RETURNED TO HER FRIENDS –

YOUR DAUGHTER IS DESTINED TO BE THE WIFE OF NONE OTHER THAN THE MIGHTY LORD SHIVA.

HOW CAN I APPROACH SHIVA? SUPPOSING HE REFUSES ME? HE HAS NOT LOOKED UPON A WOMAN SINCE SATI GAVE UP HER BODY...

...AND YET I DO NOT WISH TO SEEK FURTHER. NARADA'S PROPHECIES ALWAYS COME TRUE. I'LL WAIT AND SEE.

SO HIMAVAT WAITED. BUT ONE FINE DAY —

I HAVE WAITED LONG ENOUGH, AND SHIVA CONTINUES TO BE LOST IN MEDITATION.

SUDDENLY AN IDEA STRUCK HIM. HE WENT TO MENAKA.

I WILL SEND PARVATI TO WAIT UPON SHIVA. HE WILL NOT BE ABLE TO RESIST HER CHARMS.

AN EXCELLENT IDEA!

HIMAVAT CALLED PARVATI TO HIM.

MY BELOVED CHILD, WILL YOU, WITH YOUR FRIENDS, WAIT UPON LORD SHIVA WHO MEDITATES IN YONDER GROVE?

WE HAVE OFTEN SEEN HIM, FATHER. WE SHALL GO.

HIMAVAT TOOK PARVATI AND TWO OF HER FRIENDS AND WENT UP TO SHIVA.

LORD, YOU HAVE NONE TO HELP YOU FOR YOUR RITUALS. MY DAUGHTER CAN.

SHIVA LOOKED AT THEM CALMLY FOR A FEW SECONDS.

LET THE GIRLS SERVE ME. THEY ARE NO HINDRANCE TO ONE WHO HAS RENOUNCED THE WORLD.

THEN HE ADDRESSED HIMAVAT.

I AM GRATEFUL TO YOU FOR YOUR THOUGHTFUL GESTURE. LET THE MAIDS SERVE ME AS THEY WILL.

HIMAVAT WAS JUBILANT AS HE LEFT THE MAIDS AND WENT.

NARADA'S PROPHECY WILL COME TRUE VERY SHORTLY. I AM ASSURED OF PARVATI'S FUTURE.

PARVATI BEGAN TO ATTEND ON SHIVA.

PARVATI, HAVE YOU COLLECTED THE FLOWERS FOR TODAY'S WORSHIP?

HERE THEY ARE, MY LORD.

PARVATI, COME ON. LET US FEED THE DEER.

A MOMENT. LET ME FINISH CLEANING THE LORD'S PRAYER SEAT.

SHE CAREFULLY CHOSE THE 'KUSA' GRASS FOR HIS RITES...

COME FARTHER! THE BEST GRASS GROWS THERE.

OH! PARVATI, WE ARE TIRED.

... AND FANNED HIM GENTLY WHEN THE DAY GREW WARM.

THUS PARVATI GREW TO LOVE SHIVA WITH ALL HER HEART.

INDRA SIGNALLED TO BRIHASPATI, THEIR CHIEF PRIEST, TO SPEAK.

TARAKA, THE WICKED ASURA, HAS BECOME A MENACE.

HE HAS SEIZED HEAVEN, OUR ABODE AND IS TERRORIZING OUR PEOPLE.

INDRA STEPPED FORWARD —

I EVEN SEND HIM GIFTS TO FLATTER HIM AND WIN HIS GOODWILL.

THEN BRIHASPATI CONTINUED —

BUT THE MORE WE TRY TO PLEASE HIM THE MORE RUTHLESS HE BECOMES.

"HE HAS LAID WASTE ALL OUR BEAUTIFUL GARDENS AND OUR CAPTIVE WOMENFOLK TEARFULLY FAN HIM WHILE HE SLEEPS?"

WE HAVE COME TO ASK YOU TO GIVE US A CHIEF WHO WILL LEAD US AGAINST HIM.

BRAHMA WAS HELPLESS.

DEAR SONS, MUCH AS I WANT TO HELP YOU, I CAN'T.

TARAKA HAS BECOME POWERFUL BY VIRTUE OF THE BOON I ONCE GRANTED HIM. SO I CANNOT DESTROY HIM.

BUT HE HAD A SOLUTION.

SHIVA IS DESTINED TO MARRY PARVATI.

GO! MAKE HIM AWARE OF HER BEAUTY.

THEN BRAHMA PROMISED—

THE SON BORN AFTER THEIR WEDDING WILL BE YOUR **WAR-LORD** AND KILL TARAKA.

INDRA WENT STRAIGHT TO KAMA, THE GOD OF LOVE.

WHAT CAN I DO FOR YOU, MY LORD?

I WANT YOU TO LURE SHIVA INTO MARRYING PARVATI.

IT SHALL BE DONE.

COME RATI, MY BELOVED WIFE AND SPRING, MY BOSOM COMPANION. LET US GO TO SHIVA'S GROVE.

BUT AS THEY APPROACHED SHIVA'S GROVE AND KAMA SAW THE MIGHTY SHIVA—

MY COURAGE FAILS ME!

AT THAT MOMENT PARVATI PASSED BY AND KAMA REGAINED COURAGE.

WITH SUCH AN ALLY I CANNOT FAIL.

PARVATI BOWED AND PLACED SOME FLOWERS BEFORE SHIVA, WHO HAD JUST COME OUT OF A DIVINE TRANCE.

MAY YOU BE BLESSED, SWEET MAID, WITH A HUSBAND WHO LOVES NONE BUT YOU.

SHIVA HAS SPOKEN AND HE CANNOT LIE. I AM SO HAPPY.

PARVATI WAS ABOUT TO PLACE A LOTUS GARLAND AROUND SHIVA'S NECK WHEN ...

AH! THE TIME IS RIPE.

KAMA'S ARROW FOUND IT'S MARK.

WHAT A BEAUTIFUL CREATURE IS SHE WHO SERVES ME! WHY HAVE I NOT BEEN AWARE OF THIS?

WHY DO I BLUSH WHEN THE LORD LOOKS AT ME? I FEEL STRANGE.

BUT WITH A GREAT EFFORT SHIVA BROUGHT HIS EMOTIONS UNDER CONTROL, AND LOOKED AROUND.

WHO HAS DARED DISTURB THE PEACE IN MY SOUL?

HE SAW KAMA AND ANGER FILLED HIS BEING.

HE LOOKED AT KAMA AND THAT GOD WAS BURNT TO ASHES.

ONE LOOK AT HIM AND RATI FAINTED.

WITHOUT SO MUCH AS LOOKING AT PARVATI, SHIVA LEFT THE GROVE.

PARVATI WAS OVERCOME WITH GRIEF AND SHAME.

NOT ONLY HAVE I LOVED IN VAIN BUT MY BELOVED HAS SPURNED ME BEFORE MY PLAYMATES!

15

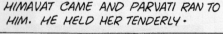

HIMAVAT CAME AND PARVATI RAN TO HIM. HE HELD HER TENDERLY.

DEAR CHILD!

FATHER.

THEY MADE THEIR WAY HOMEWARD, SLOWLY AND SADLY.

IN THE MEANWHILE RATI WOKE UP FROM HER FAINT.

OF WHAT USE IS LIFE TO ME WHEN MY KAMA IS DEAD? IT WERE BETTER I TOO DIED AND JOINED HIM.

BUT A HEAVENLY VOICE STOPPED HER.

LIVE OH WIDOWED LADY. PARVATI WILL YET WIN SHIVA BY PENANCE, AND YOUR HUSBAND WILL BE RESTORED TO YOU ON THEIR WEDDING DAY.

RATI, CONSOLED AND CHEERED BY THE VOICE, LIVED AND WAITED FOR KAMA.

PARVATI WAS EXTREMELY PAINED BY SHIVA'S BEHAVIOUR BUT SHE CONTINUED TO LOVE HIM.

MY BEAUTY HAS FAILED TO MOVE HIM.

BUT I WILL NOT GIVE UP. SHIVA MAY NOT VALUE BEAUTY BUT PENANCE AND DEVOTION WILL CERTAINLY WIN HIM.

SHE TOLD HER MOTHER OF HER DECISION.

BUT WHY, MY CHILD? ARE THERE NO GODS TO LOVE YOU HERE? GIVE HIM UP.

MOTHER, YOU CANNOT UNDERSTAND. I HAVE DECIDED. PLEASE BLESS ME.

AND MENAKA SHAKING HER HEAD BLESSED PARVATI.

PARVATI THEN WENT TO HIMAVAT.

FATHER, GIVE ME YOUR CONSENT AND A GROVE THAT I MIGHT SPEND MY DAYS IN PENANCE AND PRAYER.

SO BE IT, MY BELOVED CHILD.

CASTING OFF HER FINE CLOTHES AND JEWELLERY, PARVATI ENTERED THE GROVE HER FATHER GAVE HER.

THE DEER IN THE GROVE LOVED HER.

SHE SLEPT ON THE COLD DAMP GROUND AND BARELY ATE ANYTHING.

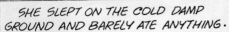

DO YOU FAIL TO UNDERSTAND MY LOVE? I DON'T BELIEVE IT. PERHAPS YOU WISH TO TRY ME FURTHER.

AS SHE PERFORMED HER RITES, THE HERMITS NEARBY OFTEN CAME TO WATCH...

...AND MARVELLED.

18

GRADUALLY SHE GAVE UP EVEN THE LITTLE SHE ATE.

SHE HAS EATEN NOTHING SINCE WEEKS.

SHE IS *APARNA

* LADY OF THE UNBROKEN FAST.

I WILL SUBSIST ON YOUR NAME RESTING ON MY LIPS.

SHE SAT IN AN ICY POOL, HER LIPS QUIVERING, AND CONCENTRATED ON HER LORD.

TRULY SHE IS THE ASCETIC OF ASCETICS.

YOUR IMAGE FIXED IN MY HEART SHALL WARM ME.

MANY YEARS PASSED BUT PARVATI NEVER ONCE GAVE UP HOPE.

ONE DAY WHILE SHE WAS PERFORMING HER RITUALS BEFORE ENTERING THE POOL, A YOUNG HERMIT CAME TO SEE HER. PARVATI BOWED TO HIM.

HOW CAN YOUR TENDER FRAME CARRY OUT THE TASK YOUR SPIRIT HAS SET IT?

19

ALL HER AUSTERITY HAD ONLY ENHANCED PARVATI'S EXQUISITE BEAUTY.

TRULY YOU HAVE PROVED TO THE WORLD THAT BEAUTY AND PURITY NEED NOT DESTROY ONE ANOTHER.

YOUR DEEDS HAVE CROWNED YOUR FATHER WITH AN EVEN GREATER GLORY THAN HE ALREADY OWNED.

NOBLE MAIDEN, WHY HAVE YOU UNDERTAKEN SUCH SEVERE PENANCE?

IT IS COMMON FOR A LONELY PERSON TORN BY GRIEF AND ANGUISH TO LIVE A HERMIT'S LIFE.

BUT WHY SHOULD YOU OH FAULTLESS ONE, LOVED AND CHERISHED BY ALL, DO SO?

HEARING THIS PARVATI HEAVED A HEAVY SIGH.

AH! IS IT BECAUSE OF UNREQUITED LOVE? NO, THAT'S NOT POSSIBLE. A PRICELESS GEM LIKE YOU IS SOUGHT AND DOES NOT SEEK.

GO HOME FAIR MAIDEN. I WILL GIVE YOU HALF THE MERITS I'VE EARNED IF YOU STOP THIS PENANCE. BUT PRAY TELL ME THE REASON.

PARVATI TURNED TO HER FRIEND FOR HELP.

THE MAID TOLD ALL.

SHE HAD SET HER HEART ON WINNING SHIVA'S LOVE. SHE FAILED TO WIN HIM BY HER BEAUTY. SO SHE DECIDED TO DO IT BY PENANCE AND AUSTERITY.

SHE OFTEN CRIES OUT TO HIM BUT SHIVA HAS REMAINED DEAF TO HER APPEALS.

THE HERMIT TURNED TO PARVATI.

IS THIS TRUE? OR IS YOUR FRIEND JOKING?

OH HOLY ONE, IT IS TRUE! I ADORE GREAT SHIVA. I AM SURE, I WILL WIN HIS LOVE BY MY PENANCE AND DEVOTION.

LOW CREATURES CAN NEVER UNDERSTAND LOFTY MOTIVES. YOUR TONGUE GIVES AWAY YOUR EVIL MIND.

SHIVA NEITHER IMPRESSES NOR IS IMPRESSED BY OUTWARD APPEARANCES. HIS VALUES ARE DIFFERENT FROM YOURS.

WHAT IF HE IS UNCOUTH POOR AND ILL-CLAD? WHAT IF SERPENTS DECK HIS BODY? HE IS MY CHOSEN LORD.

HIS FAILINGS MAY BE MANY AND HIS VIRTUES FEW, BUT I LOVE HIM.

THEN PARVATI TURNED TO HER FRIEND WHO LISTENED IN AWE.

DEAR MAID, ASK HIM TO GO AWAY. WHY SHOULD HE DEFILE HIS HEART WITH SUCH SLANDER?

BESIDES, THOUGH IT IS A SIN TO UTTER EVIL WORDS IT IS A GREATER SIN TO WAIT AND LISTEN. COME LET US GO.

AS PARVATI TURNED ANGRILY AWAY...

..THE HERMIT RUSHED FORWARD AND BLOCKED HER PATH.

PARVATI WAS PARALYSED WITH SURPRISE. THE HERMIT WAS NONE OTHER THAN HER DEAR LORD, SHIVA.

OH ! GENTLE MAIDEN, YOUR PENANCE AND DEVOTION HAVE WON ME. I BOW TO YOU, YOUR WILLING SLAVE.

BUT PARVATI, THE EVER DUTIFUL, LEFT SHIVA AND WENT TO HER FRIEND.

TELL HIM THAT MY FATHER SHOULD BE APPROACHED FOR MY HAND.

26

THE MAID DID SO AND PARVATI CAME BACK TO SHIVA.

DEAR ONE, I SHALL LOSE NO TIME.

THUS ASSURED, PARVATI WITH HER FRIEND TURNED HOMEWARD.

SHIVA CALLED FOR THE SEVEN RISHIS.

BRAHMA HAS PROMISED THE GODS THAT MY SON SHALL LEAD THEM AGAINST TARAKA.

TO FULFIL HIS PROMISE I WISH TO MARRY PARVATI. GO AND ASK HIMAVAT FOR HER HAND.

HIMAVAT OF COURSE WAS DELIGHTED.

AND THE WEDDING TOOK PLACE.

WHEN THE CEREMONY WAS OVER, THE GODS CAME TO SHIVA.

WE BEG YOU TO RESTORE KAMA TO RATI. FOR THE SAKE OF YOUR LOVELY BRIDE, HAVE PITY ON THE TENDER GOD AND HIS MOURNING WIFE.

I WILL. AM I NOT KAMA'S SLAVE TOO, NOW?

MANY YEARS PASSED AND SHIVA WAS LOST IN HIS LOVE FOR HIS WIFE.

SO INDRA SENT AGNI TO SHIVA.

I HAVE COME TO REMIND YOU OF OUR NEED.

SHIVA GAVE AGNI A SEED IN HIS PALM.

WHEN THIS IS RIPE A CHILD WILL EMERGE HE SHALL BE YOUR WAR-LORD.

AGNI TOOK THE SEED BUT IT WAS SO HOT, HE COULD BARELY HOLD IT.

I MUST HASTEN TO INDRA.

BY THE TIME HE REACHED INDRA, HE BECAME PALE WITH DISCOMFORT.

I HAVE IT BUT I CAN NO LONGER BEAR IT.

INDRA FELT SORRY FOR HIM.

TAKE IT TO GANGA. SHE WILL COOL YOU AS WELL AS SUSTAIN IT.

AGNI WENT TO GANGA. BUT WHEN HE DIPPED HIMSELF AND THE SEED IN HER COOL WATERS, SHE BUBBLED AND BOILED OVER, AND THE SEED WAS THROWN ASHORE.

JUST THEN SIX CELESTIAL NYMPHS CAME TO BATHE IN THE GANGA.

WHAT IS THIS? A SEED?

LET US LAY IT IN A NEST OF SHARA GRASS.

THEY PICKED THE SEED AND PLACED IT NEAR SOME 'SHARA' GRASS.

THE SEED AT THAT MOMENT WAS RIPE AND KARTIKEYA EMERGED. THE CHILD GREW SIX FACES TO CHUCKLE AT EACH OF THE SIX NYMPHS WHO GAZED AT IT IN WONDER.

WE SHALL TAKE HIM WITH US. WE SAW HIM FIRST.

JUST THEN GANGA CAME OUT IN THE FORM OF A WOMAN AND AGNI TOO APPEARED.

I WILL TAKE HIM. I BORE HIM.

NO! HE IS PROMISED TO US.

AT THAT MOMENT SHIVA AND PARVATI REACHED THE SCENE. SHIVA SETTLED THE MATTER.

WHO ELSE BUT PARVATI IS THE FIT ONE TO BRING UP A CHILD DESTINED TO LEAD THE GODS?

PARVATI PICKED THE CHILD UP TENDERLY AND CLASPED IT TO HER.

AND LED BY SHIVA RETURNED TO MOUNT KAILAS.

IN TIME KARTIKEYA GREW UP AND LED THE GODS IN A FIERCE BATTLE AGAINST THE EVIL TARAKA AND SLEW HIM.

INDRA WAS RESTORED TO THE THRONE, AND HAPPINESS REIGNED ONCE MORE IN HEAVEN.